CLASSIC CLIP ART

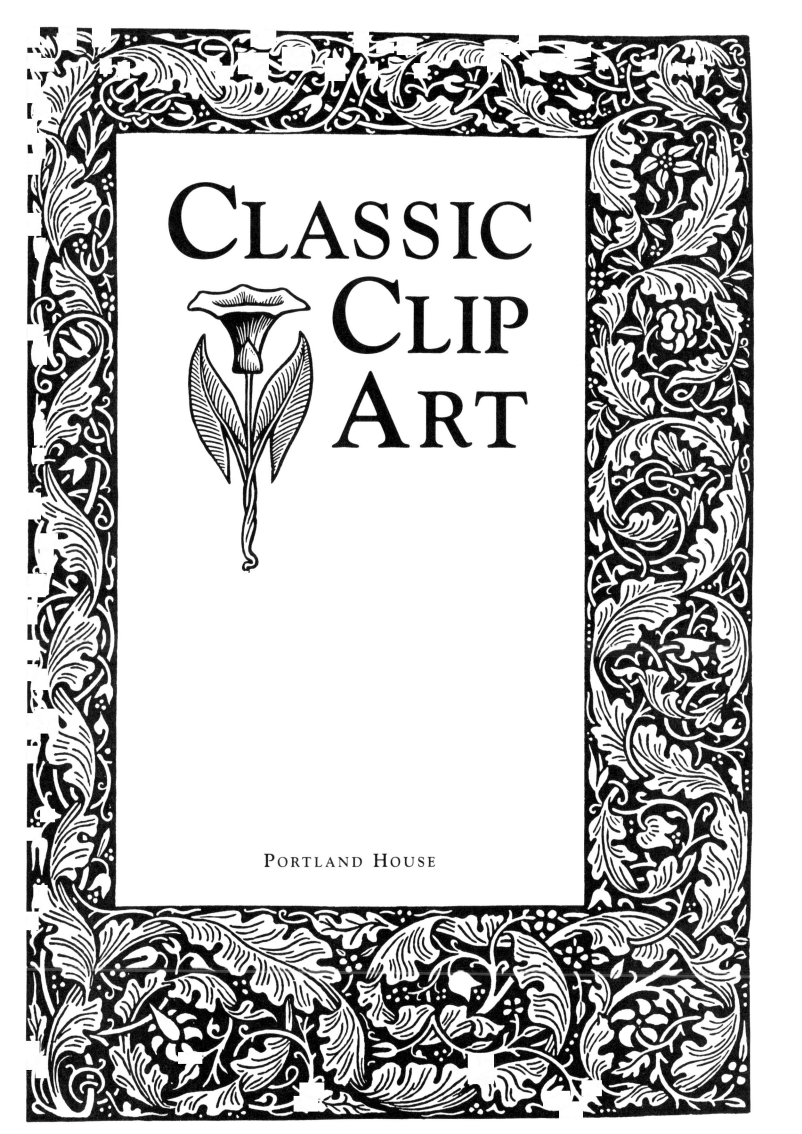

CLASSIC CLIP ART

PORTLAND HOUSE

This 1997 edition is published by Portland House,
a division of Random House Value Publishing, Inc.,
201 East 50th Street, New York, New York 10022

Printed and bound in the United States of America

ISBN 0-517-20199-2

8 7 6 5 4 3 2 1

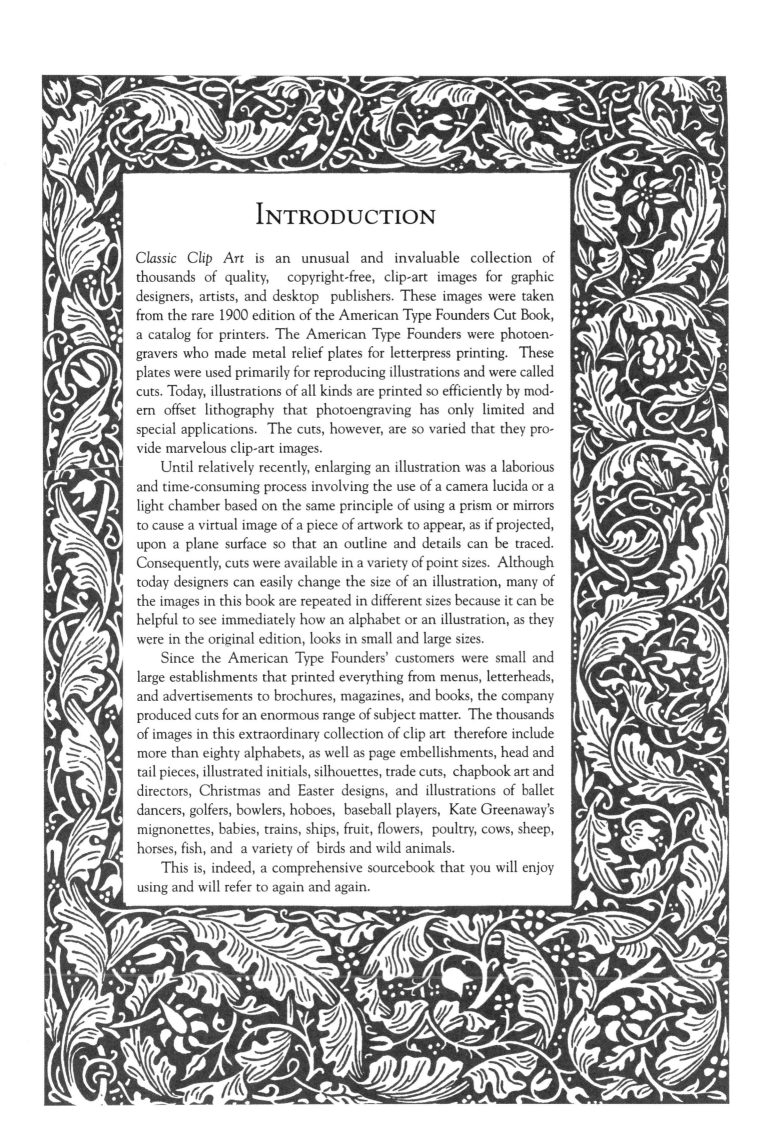

INTRODUCTION

Classic Clip Art is an unusual and invaluable collection of thousands of quality, copyright-free, clip-art images for graphic designers, artists, and desktop publishers. These images were taken from the rare 1900 edition of the American Type Founders Cut Book, a catalog for printers. The American Type Founders were photoengravers who made metal relief plates for letterpress printing. These plates were used primarily for reproducing illustrations and were called cuts. Today, illustrations of all kinds are printed so efficiently by modern offset lithography that photoengraving has only limited and special applications. The cuts, however, are so varied that they provide marvelous clip-art images.

Until relatively recently, enlarging an illustration was a laborious and time-consuming process involving the use of a camera lucida or a light chamber based on the same principle of using a prism or mirrors to cause a virtual image of a piece of artwork to appear, as if projected, upon a plane surface so that an outline and details can be traced. Consequently, cuts were available in a variety of point sizes. Although today designers can easily change the size of an illustration, many of the images in this book are repeated in different sizes because it can be helpful to see immediately how an alphabet or an illustration, as they were in the original edition, looks in small and large sizes.

Since the American Type Founders' customers were small and large establishments that printed everything from menus, letterheads, and advertisements to brochures, magazines, and books, the company produced cuts for an enormous range of subject matter. The thousands of images in this extraordinary collection of clip art therefore include more than eighty alphabets, as well as page embellishments, head and tail pieces, illustrated initials, silhouettes, trade cuts, chapbook art and directors, Christmas and Easter designs, and illustrations of ballet dancers, golfers, bowlers, hoboes, baseball players, Kate Greenaway's mignonettes, babies, trains, ships, fruit, flowers, poultry, cows, sheep, horses, fish, and a variety of birds and wild animals.

This is, indeed, a comprehensive sourcebook that you will enjoy using and will refer to again and again.

MORRIS SERIES, 77

MORRIS SERIES, 78

JENSON SERIES, 80

JENSON SERIES, 82

The letters of the alphabet not shown are uniform in style with those of Jenson Series 80

WAYSIDE SERIES, 1

HAPGOOD SERIES, 1

72 POINT EMPIRE SERIES

48 POINT EMPIRE SERIES

IPSEN SERIES, 1

A A B C D E
F G H I J K L M N O P
Q R S T U V W X Y Z

IPSEN SERIES, 2

A A B C D E F G H I J K L M
N O P Q R S T U V W X Y Z

42 POINT BRADLEY SERIES

48 POINT SCHOEFFER OLD STYLE SERIES

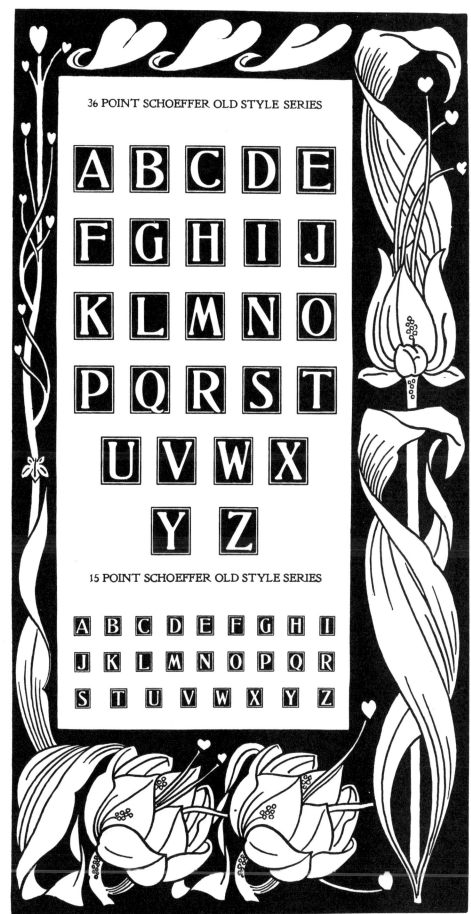

36 POINT SCHOEFFER OLD STYLE SERIES

15 POINT SCHOEFFER OLD STYLE SERIES

RENATE SERIES, 69

RENATE SERIES, 70

WAVERLEY INITIALS, 74

A B C D E
F G H I J K L
M N O P Q R S
T U V W X Y Z

ACORN SERIES, 71

A B C D E
F G H I J
K L M N O
P Q R S T
U V W X Y

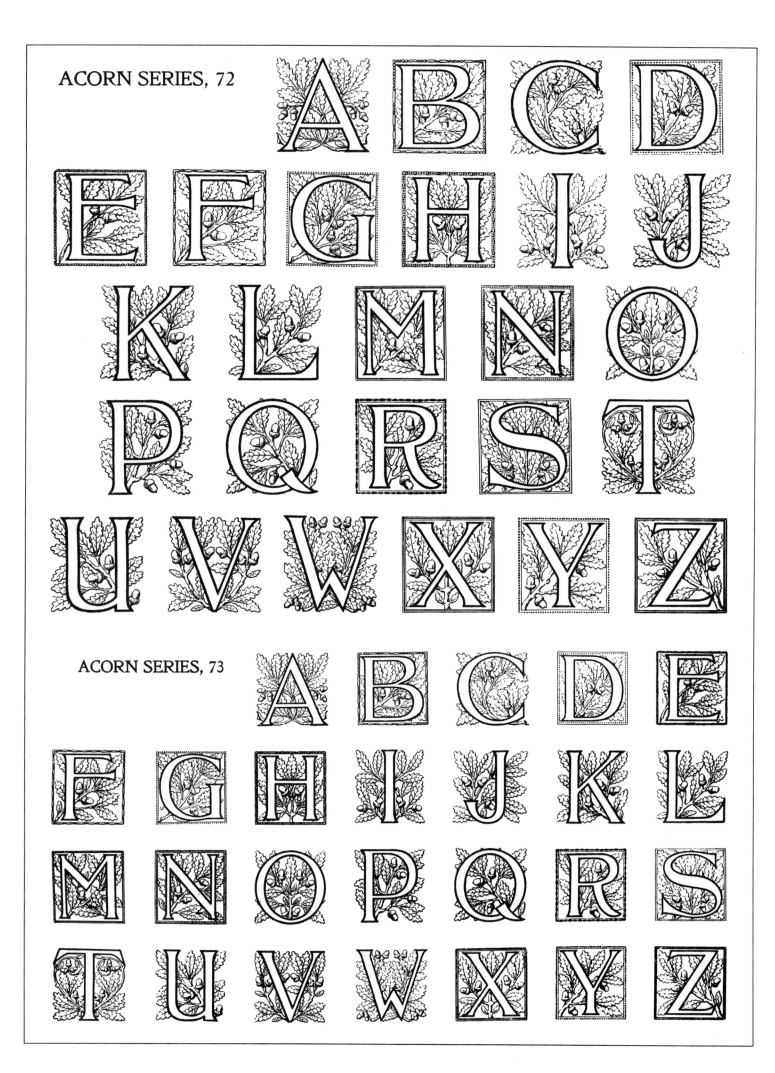

ACORN SERIES, 72

ACORN SERIES, 73

GAIETE SERIES, 55

GAIETE SERIES, 54

NEPTUNE SERIES, 65

A B C D E
F G H I J K
L M N O P Q R S
T U V W X Y Z

NEPTUNE SERIES, 66

A B C D E F G H I
J K L M N O P Q R
S T U V W X Y Z

KOSMO SERIES, 67

A B C D E

F G H I J K L

M N O P Q R S

T U V W X Y Z

KOSMO SERIES, 58

A B C D E F G H

I K L M N O P Q R

S T U V W X Y Z

NONAME SERIES, 59

A B C D E

F G H I J K L

M N O P Q R S

T U V W X Y Z

NONAME SERIES, 60

A B C D E F G H I

J K L M N O P R

S T U V W X Y Z

MISSAL SERIES, 58

LENTEN SERIES, 50

LENTEN SERIES, 51

BEAUISH SERIES, 63

BEAUISH SERIES, 64

MULTIPLE SERIES, 53

MULTIPLE SERIES, 52

FLORAL SERIES, 61

FLORAL SERIES, 62

TENDRIL SERIES, 1

A A B C D E F G H
I J K L M M N O P
Q R S S T
U V W
Y X Z

TENDRIL SERIES, 2

A B C D E
F G H I J
K L M M
N O P Q R
S S T U V
W X Y Z

SERIES 321 — Ornamented

SERIES 320 — Ornamented

INDEX SERIES, 1

INDEX SERIES, 2

72 POINT ART SERIES

48 POINT ART SERIES

ABCDAFGHIJKLM
NOPQRSTUVWXYZ

ABCDEFGH
IJKLMNOPQRSTUV
WXYZ

ABCDEFGH
IJKLMNOPQRSTUV
WXYZ

ABCDEFGHIJK
LMNOPQRSTUV

ABCDEF
GHIJKLMNO
PQRSTUV

ABCDEF
GHIJKLMNO
PQRSTUV
WXYZ

ABCDEFGH
IJKLMNOP

SERIES 1159

A B C D E F

THIRTY-FOURTH SERIES

A B C D E

SERIES 1158

A B C D

SERIES 426

A B C D E G H I J

BUSHA ORNAMENTS

SECTIONAL INITIALS

These Initials are made in five pieces; and can be combined to make various lengths as desired

B **S** **A**

U   **H**

43

BUSHA ORNAMENTS

BUSHA ORNAMENTS

BUSHA ORNAMENTS

BUSHA ORNAMENTS

DELLA ROBBIA INITIALS

ILLUSTRATED INITIALS

Boxing

Golf

Fire Scene

Rowing

Running

Tennis

Golf

Winter

Base Ball

Boxing

Men-of-War

Fire Scene

Music

Tennis

Golf

Cycling

Music

Men-of-War

Fire Scene

Running

Boxing

Winter

Cycling

Winter

Tennis

Music

Base Ball

BASEBALL SPECIALS

MORTISED INITIAL SQUARES

"WOOD-CUT" MORTISED INITIAL SQUARES

BUSHA MORTISED INITIALS

STRATHMORE INITIALS

ROYCROFT INITIALS

MOTHER GOOSE INITIALS

ABCDEFGHIJKLMNOPQRSTUVWXYZ

ABCDEFGHIJKLMNOPQRST
UVWXYZ

ABCDEFGHIJKLMNO
PQRSTUVWXYZ

ABCDEFGHIJK
LMNOPQRST
UVWXYZ

ABCDEFGHIJO
PQRSTUVW

ABCDEFGE
LMNOP

ATREAM

POST OLD STYLE ORNAMENTS

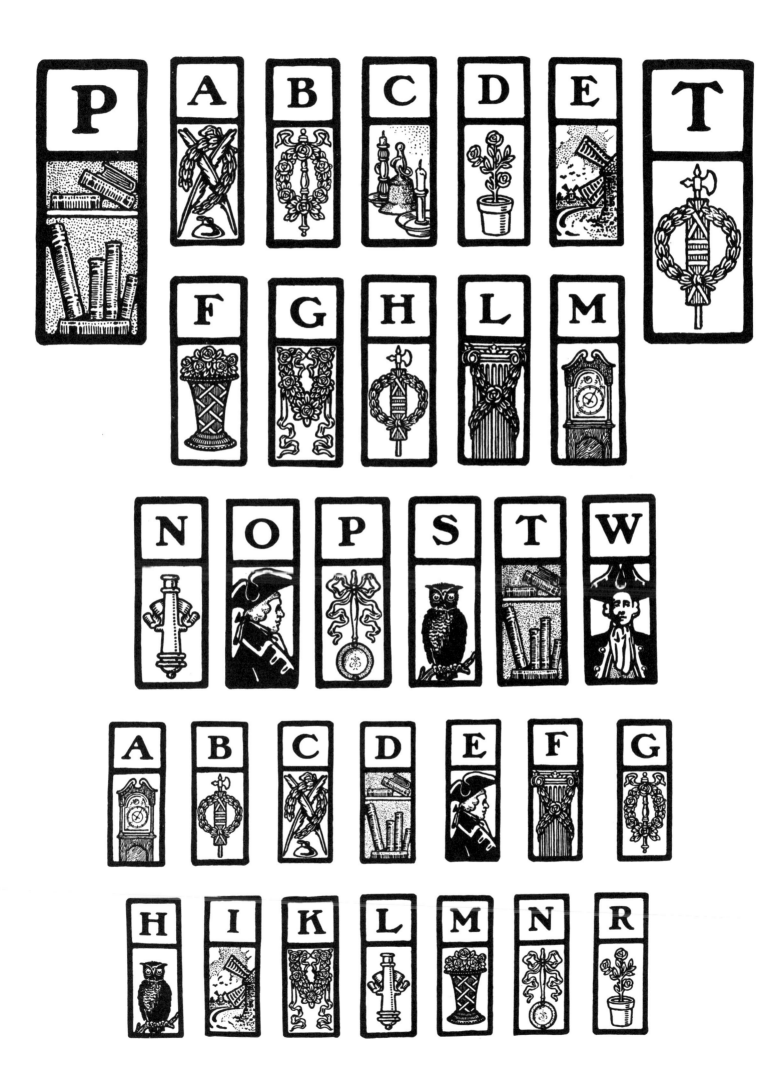

POST OLD STYLE ORNAMENTS

POST OLD STYLE ORNAMENTS

FLORAL PANELS

DELLA ROBBIA ORNAMENTS

DELLA ROBBIA COMBINATION ORNAMENTS

GRASSET ORNAMENTS

GRASSET ORNAMENTS

RENAISSANCE ORNAMENTS

RENAISSANCE INITIALS

FLOWERS AND FRUIT

CHECK ORNAMENTS

7½
$$\frac{3.8}{21.7.6}$$
6/16

STRATHMORE ORNAMENTS

LAUREL WREATHS

ELECTROTYPED BACKGROUNDS

Bought of

ELECTROTYPED BACKGROUNDS

ELECTROTYPED BACKGROUNDS

TOURAINE SERIES ELECTROTYPE CUTS

DELMONICO'S CHEFS AND WAITERS

MASCOTS

INSECTS

PICK-UPS

SILHOUETTES

LISTENERS

HOBOES

SPEAKERS

KLONDIKERS

COPPERS

DRUGGISTS

SHOPPERS

GOLFERS

DOMESTICS

GOLFERS No. 2

CAMPAIGNERS

BALLET DANCERS

HOBOES

KLONDIKERS

SHOPPERS

GOLFERS

LADY SPEAKERS

SCORCHERS

GOLFERS

ARMY AND NAVY No. 1

ARMY AND NAVY No. 2

BOWLERS

KATE GREENAWAY'S MIGNONETTES

TOURAINE SERIES ELECTROTYPE CUTS

MENU ELECTROTYPE CUTS

TRADE CUTS

RELIGIOUS EMBLEMS

MALTESE CROSSES, STARS, ETC.

RELIGIOUS EMBLEMS—Christian Endeavor, Epworth League, Etc.

SOCIETY EMBLEMS—Masonic

SOCIETY EMBLEMS

ELECTROTYPED EAGLES

FIRE ENGINES, LOCOMOTIVES, ETC.

STEAMBOATS, SHIPS, ETC.

TRADE CUTS, CARRIAGES, ETC.

MISCELLANEOUS CUTS, INITIALS, ETC.

MISCELLANEOUS CUTS

ELECTROTYPED FISTS, STARS, ETC.

MISCELLANEOUS CUTS

MISCELLANEOUS CUTS

MISCELLANEOUS CUTS

MISCELLANEOUS CUTS

FOR CHRIST AND THE CHURCH

COLUMBUS. 1492.

MISCELLANEOUS CUTS

MISCELLANEOUS CUTS

TROUSERS

HEY, THERE!

A WORD WITH YOU SIR!

PRINTERS

24×30

SOUVENIR

ALONG THE LINE

LIVERY

MISCELLANEOUS CUTS

CIRCLES, SEALS, ETC.

CARD PIPS

ELECTRO OUTLINE FIGURES, ETC.

CHRISTMAS HOLIDAY CUTS AND MURAL ORNAMENTS

MISCELLANEOUS CUTS

CALENDAR ELECTROS

Chap-Book Directors

CHAP-BOOK CUTS

CHAP-BOOK CUTS

CHAP-BOOK CUTS

TWENTIETH CENTURY ORNAMENTS

TWENTIETH CENTURY ORNAMENTS

MISSION TOYS

BULFINCH ATTRACTORS

A series of pictures for attracting the eye and arousing the interest, thereby increasing the value of printed matter. They are intended to illustrate catchy phrases (a million or more of which are applicable), a few of which are printed.

No Use Talking

Just a Coaxer

It's Got to Go

Can't be Beat

Lest You Forget

There's No Time

Don't be Foolish

Read it Through

Think it Over

Nothing Doing

Always Ahead

Out of Order

There's No Kick Coming

Our Claims are Stronger

Our Prices Can't be Beat

Entwine a Piece of String

Our Time is Your Time

It is Very, Very Simple

Send for Booklet

After Due Consideration

Have You Become Weary

Write Us and We'll Call

DELLA ROBBIA WORD TERMINALS

TRADE CUTS

TRADE CUTS

HELLO CUTS

ELEPHANTS, HORSES, PIGS, ETC.

HORSES

HORSES

ELECTROTYPES OF HORSES

AUTOMOBILES AND HORSES

HORSES AND CATTLE

5697A 30 cts.

HORSES, ETC.

HORSES AND CATTLE

CATTLE

CATTLE

CATTLE, SHEEP, PIGS AND RABBITS

POULTRY

CATTLE AND SHEEP

SHEEP

PIGS

DOGS

DOGS

DOGS, ETC.

POULTRY

POULTRY

POULTRY

POULTRY

POULTRY

POULTRY

POULTRY

POULTRY

POULTRY

TURKEYS

DUCKS ETC.

POULTRY (Continued), FISH, CRUSTACEA, FISHING TACKLE, ETC.

FISH, CRUSTACEA, ETC.

ANIMALS

ANIMALS

PIGEONS

BIRDS